Contents

SCHERKENBACH
ELEMENTARY SCHOOL

Improving Your Story Writing

Do you want to improve your story writing? A good way is to learn strategies used by successful story writers. How do published writers compose their stories?

- How do they add interest to story beginnings?
- How do they effectively portray emotions?
- How do they develop a unique storyteller's voice?
- How do they write memorable endings?

Begin by considering the central question: "What strategies do I use when I write stories?" The more specific strategies you can identify, the more likely you are to use them in your story writing.

Use the Strategy Checklist on page 27 to mark the strategies you already use in your story writing. If you are not sure about the meaning of an item on the list, mark it with a question mark. After working through this book, return to the checklist to see if you are using the strategies you have learned.

Setting Writing Goals

Your response to the checklist on page 27 will help you set an immediate goal — the strategy that is your priority to improve your story writing. Once you achieve a specific goal in your writing, choose another strategy as your goal. Remember that you don't need to write a new story each time you focus on a new strategy. Why not use the strategy to revise a story you have already written? While you may revise the same story many times, each revision should focus on the strategy that is your current goal.

Consider keeping a goals chart in your writing folder or binder. See page 28 for a graphic organizer you can use. Useful in conferences with your teacher and others, the chart records your dated list of what you need to improve in your writing as well as a dated notation about when you demonstrate the improvement.

Sample of a Goals Chart

My Personal Writing Goals	
Goals Identified	**Goals Achieved**
– add more showing not telling (Sept) – improve wordy, clumsy sentences (Sept)	– Oct 14: story included showing – Oct 27: description improved

	Expectations	Strategies
Organization	Your story clearly establishes a conflict that is resolved. The beginning and ending command attention. You effectively employ transitions.	1, 2, 3, 11, 12
Content	Your writing is understandable and interesting. Details stay focused on the story's conflict.	3, 4, 5, 6, 9, 11, 12
Sentence Structure	Your sentences are complete and varied in construction.	7, 11, 12
Vocabulary	Your word choice is precise and colorful (e.g., "staggered" instead of "walked").	8, 11, 12
Voice	Your story makes use of original content and language. You include details others might overlook with original but appropriate word choice and comparisons.	4, 8, 9, 11, 12
Conventions	Your spelling, usage, and punctuation are correct; you avoid errors that confuse and distract the reader.	10, 11, 12

USING RUBRICS TO TRACK IMPROVEMENT

The twelve strategies explained in this book relate directly to rubrics you and your teacher probably use to assess your writing. Rubrics identify critical writing expectations achieved by successful writers. Typically, rubrics for story writing specify expectations for content, organization, sentence structure, vocabulary, voice, and conventions.

USING STORY WRITING STRATEGIES

1 Writing Variables for Stories

Whether you are creating a story or writing in another form, the RAFTS variables will help you achieve success. Think about RAFTS variables before you begin planning and drafting your story to gain these advantages:

- You remind yourself about what is required in your writing.
- You efficiently consider your options.
- You discover valuable ideas for your writing.

RAFTS Variables

R = Role: From whose point of view am I writing?
A = Audience: To whom am I writing?
F = Format: What type of writing am I completing?
T = Topic: What am I writing about?
S = Strong Purpose: What is my purpose?

Action Plan

1. Choose a favorite published story and analyze the writing variables: the Role of the narrator, the Audience for the story, the Format (a story), the Topic, and the Strong Purpose or theme suggested by the story.
2. Apply the RAFTS variables to a story that you are planning to write. If you are completing a writing assignment, determine the variables that are assigned (often the Topic). Remember that if a variable is not assigned, you should consider it carefully and make a choice.
3. **Test Strategy**: Write the word *RAFTS* right by the test assignment to focus on your writing task and to review test requirements. Write a brief note for each item: your role, your audience, your format, your topic, and your strong purpose.

ROLE

What is the difference between the two story beginnings shown here?

> Tim and his dad planned their river kayaking trips for weeks. Their excitement turned to fear seconds after they launched their kayaks. Tim yelled to his father, "Dad, the water is too high!"
> *Or*
> "Dad, the water is too high!" But my voice drowned in the thrashing sounds of the enormous rapids. Straining, I forced myself to paddle to reach my destination safely.

In the first example in the box, the author is in the role of storyteller. In the second example, a character in the story tells the story in the first person (in grammar, "I" and "we" are labeled *first-person*). Often it is easier for student writers to write in the first person. The role reminds them to use their own experiences as they develop the main character's conflict. The role also helps them write in a familiar voice (for more on Voice, see page 20).

AUDIENCE

Student writers often choose people their own age as audience for their stories. Think about your classmates and what you could help them understand about themselves.

FORMAT

Read examples of writing in your selected or assigned writing format. Don't forget to read stories written by students as well as professional authors.

> Here are some collections to remind you what is possible when you write stories:
>
> *Golden Girls and Other Stories*, Gillian Chan
> *Athletic Shorts*, Chris Crutcher
> *Back of Beyond*, Sarah Ellis
> *A Walk in My World: International stories about youth*
> *Finding Our Way*, Rene Saldana
> *Lord of the Fries and Other Stories*, Tim Wynne-Jones
>
> You might also read magazines that include stories by young writers. Examples include *Stone Soup* and *The Claremount Review*.

Your central character's problem or conflict is the most critical element in your story. In fact, your character's conflict is what your story is about — it's your topic. What is the conflict? How will your character handle the conflict? How will the conflict be resolved?

An overall plan for writing will encourage you to elaborate on details related to your story's conflict. For now, remember that without a conflict, you have no story. The excerpt shown here presents clearly the story's conflict — a young swimmer's doubt about being able to complete a swimming race.

Finally the time came. I tentatively approached poolside. I stepped up, pulled my goggles down and nervously readjusted them. The goal: to swim one mile — 64 impossible lengths. My prognosis: NEVER! But I knew I had to try.

The most valuable stories are those that challenge readers to think about their lives, to understand something about themselves. We call these understandings or insights the themes of a story. Here are a few tips for making sure your story has a strong theme:

- It might help to remember that effective story writers *suggest* rather than *preach* their themes.
- See page 10 for strategies for writing story endings to suggest a theme.
- Student writers often base their stories on an action movie, TV show, or video game. This is often not a good choice, as stories with plenty of action usually fail to help readers understand something about themselves.

For other strategies related to Organization, see Revision that Works on page 24 and Sharing Your Story on page 25.

2 Story Beginnings that Command Attention

Interesting stories feature interesting openings, beginnings that command attention. Learn about options used by successful story writers before you select the technique that will work most effectively in your story.

Here are a few examples of how student writers use effective story beginnings:

- Plunge the reader into a conflict or dramatic event.

  There I was, helpless, frightened and stranded. As I glanced around the darkening school ground, I saw them — my attackers. I glanced furtively for my friends. They had vanished. I backed up slowly until I was cornered between the climbing bars and the swings. I smiled as they approached but I churned inside.

- Present a brief monologue or dialogue related to the conflict.

  There I was lost and bleeding under the blistering hot sun of the desert. I had just escaped from prison. My stomach rumbled with hunger pains. Night was looming and I had nowhere to hide.

- Describe a setting with a focus on movement or action.

  She sat on a little corner against a brick wall beside an alley. Shoppers passed. She tried to hide from their hustle and bustle. She wanted to reach out her hand to beg but she could only look down to the dirty pavement.

- Introduce suspense to make the reader wonder.

  It was the Friday afternoon of the last day of Christmas vacation. The house sat silent as everyone relaxed. The telephone ring broke the silence. My mother took the call. Our eyes bugged out and we scattered when she announced, "One of you has to baby-sit for the Gibleys tonight."

Action Plan

1. Review two or three published stories to analyze how the author begins the story.
2. Use one of the four techniques on this page to begin your own story.
3. Rewrite the beginning of a story to make it more interesting.

3 Endings that Point to Theme

Story endings often illustrate what has changed in the main character's life. Sometimes story endings show how the main character has made someone else's life different. In focusing on what is different in a character's life, writers use endings to imply a theme, a new understanding or insight for the reader.

While all of the story's elements — conflict, rising action, and resolution — relate to the theme, it is the ending that leaves the reader with the most powerful suggestion of the theme.

> ### Tips for Effective Story Endings
> - Successful stories suggest a theme without preaching.
> - Avoid endings like "The moral of the story is …" or "It all goes to show that…"
> - Always avoid cop-out endings, such as making the whole story a dream. Cop-out endings never suggest a theme as effectively as endings that provide a realistic resolution following the climax.

When you read your favorite published writers, check out how they use story endings to suggest a theme. You will notice that they show what is different by using techniques like these:

- Conclude with a surprising twist. The "something different" is the difference between what is expected and what occurs — a form of irony.
Example: A little girl is lost at the carnival. Her frantic mother searches everywhere and seeks volunteers to help. After an hour, the mother finds her little girl sitting under a tree eating an ice-cream cone.

   "Mommy, I'm so glad they found you!" the little girl shouted.
   "What do you mean, found ME?"
   "Mommy, I went to get my ice cream. Too bad you got lost."

- Tell about a final emotional response, a reaction, or something learned from the experience.
Example: Two brothers see a bear in the distance as they walk to their country school. While they reach the school safely, their journey back home is different.

> We stopped several times, looked all around and listened. Then we ran again and did not stop running until we reached our door.

- Illustrate a change in attitudes or beliefs.
Example: A seven-year-old girl wants a special doll for Christmas, and is sure Santa will bring it. When she finds the doll with a price tag affixed, she realizes that her parents supplied Santa's gifts at great sacrifice.

> The Christmas when I was seven years old was the year that I discovered the real meaning of Christmas.

- Illustrate how events might affect the protagonist's future.
Example: A teenager's best friend changes. When the friend posts nasty comments on the Internet, the teenager realizes that the friendship is over.

> Time has passed and there have been new friends. But not a new best friend. At least not for me.

Action Plan

1. For a favorite published story, indicate the technique used by the writer to end the story. Identify a theme suggested by the ending.
2. Decide on a technique that you will use to write or rewrite the ending to one of your stories. Focus on what has changed for a character, and use that to suggest the story's theme.
3. **Test Strategy**: Many students fail to include an effective ending when they write a story under test conditions. You are more likely to include a strong ending if you take time to plan your story. In the Story Frame on page 29, the *Then* prompt reminds you to present how something has changed following the climax of the story.

For other strategies related to Organization, see Revision that Works on page 24 and Sharing Your Story on page 25.

ORGANIZATION

4 Journal Writing Focused on Conflict

Journal writing will help you discover and refine ideas that you can develop in your story writing. Through journal writing, you explore your thinking and consider possibilities for stories, as well as for other writing forms such as poems, editorials, and essays.

Remember that a story always focuses on how individuals deal with conflict. When you use journal writing to explore your own conflicts and the conflicts of other people, you may discover rich possibilities as well as specific content for your story writing. Use journal writing to explore the following questions:

- What was my problem or conflict?
- How did I immediately act or react when I realized I had a problem or conflict?
- What did I think about before I decided what to do about the problem?
- What actions did I consider?
- What choice did I make?
- What choice do I wish I had made?
- What was the consequence of my choice?

Conflict can be serious — you may write about dealing with someone's insults, coping with an illness, the pressures of succeeding in school, feeling frightened, being lonely, or witnessing an accident or a crime. You might also deal with life's lighter issues, such as being locked out of your house, being stuck with a dead battery, training your stubborn dog to do tricks, or dropping your wallet down the storm sewer.

You may use journal writing to consider the conflicts of your friends as well as your own. Even if you do not shape your journal writing into a story, you will probably find that writing to explore life's conflicts deepens your understanding of the related challenges.

Action Plan

1. Pretend to be the protagonist or main character of a story you have recently read. Answer the questions at left in the role of that character.
2. Use the questions to complete journal entries focused on conflicts — your own conflicts and those of others.

5 Showing, Not Telling

Showing rather than telling represents one of the surest ways to add value to your story. Locate a part of your story in which you describe a character feeling an emotion. Do you use such words as "joy," "fear," "anger," "relief," "hatred," "jealousy," "love," "pity," or "excitement"? These words identify an emotion — telling the reader how the character feels. But how can your character "show" the emotion? Use the following list to identify details that might show the emotion you are writing about:

- your character's hair, eyes, mouth
- sounds and movements made by your character
- something your character says and how it is said
- your character's breathing and heartbeat
- your character's actions

Notice how this excerpt from a student story improves on simply telling that the main character was surprised.

> He opened his lunchbox quickly. He couldn't believe what he saw. His eyes popped out! He yelled! He nearly fell off his chair! There was a mouse peeking out of his lunchbox.

Building Suspense

Building suspense offers an opportunity to show rather than tell. Offer hints that something is wrong before you introduce the conflict. In this excerpt, the student writer hints that the baby fox is lost.

> One day the baby fox wandered off to play and he scampered too far from his home. When it was time to return, he stopped. None of the trees looked familiar. He shuddered. He looked for a path but couldn't find one. He screamed!

Action Plan

1. In a favorite published story, find a point of emotional intensity. How does the writer show the emotion?
2. Identify a place in your own story where your character has an emotional response. Add three details to show the emotion.
3. Identify the place in your own story where you establish your character's conflict. Add three details to hint that something is wrong.

6 Planning Strategies for Story Writing

Successful story writers are able to identify specific strategies that help them plan their writing. When planning your story, remember to consider some critical story elements:

- Your story needs at least one character.
- The character faces a conflict.
- The story shows how the character deals with the conflict.
- The conflict is resolved.
- The story ends with an indication of what is different in the character's life or how the story has affected others.

Writers get into trouble when they ignore these important story elements.

- For student writers, brainstorming that does not attend to story elements is always inadequate.
- You may compose a "bed to bed" story, simply outlining events that occur from the time we get up until we go back to bed. Without focus on a specific conflict, you have no story.
- When the details in your story fail to relate to the conflict, you lose focus and your story loses value.

- Many student writers include lengthy dialogue that is totally unrelated to the conflict. Dialogue unrelated to conflict distracts the reader.

Action Plan

1. Use the Story Frame (page 29) or a similar planning form to note important narrative elements in a story you have recently read.
2. Use the Story Frame (page 29) to plan your own story. If you are a visual learner, you might imagine or sketch pictures related to each element.
3. **Test Strategy:** When you are required to compose a story under time constraints on an assigned topic or prompt, remember to plan your story. You will use your time much more efficiently if you do. Your quick recall of the prompts for story elements on page 15 (*Somebody/Somewhere/ Wanted/But/Showing the problem/So/Then*) will be useful in your planning.

Using a Story Frame

Note how the Story Frame (see template on page 29) helps you think about critically important story elements in a story you have read. It can also work as a tool to plan your own story. Use the prompts to identify the story elements:

- *Somebody*: The main character or protagonist in your story.
- *Somewhere*: Where and when your story takes place.
- *Wanted*: Your main character's plans at the beginning of the story.
- *But*: The problem or conflict your main character must deal with.
- *Showing the problem*: Effects of the problem or conflict on the protagonist.
- *So*: The resolution of the problem or conflict.
- *Then*: The story's ending that shows what is different in the protagonist's life.

For other strategies that relate to Content, see Endings That Point to Theme on page 10; Writing With Voice on page 20; Revision that Works on page 24; and Sharing Your Story on page 25.

Story Frame

Title: "Bear Tracks"
Somebody —
a ten-year-old boy
Somewhere —
on his way to a country school a mile from home a hundred years ago
Wanted —
He wanted to get to school but was in no hurry.
But —
He spotted bear tracks and then saw a bear in the distance.
Showing the problem —
He shook. He dropped his lunch pail. He ran quickly to school.
So —
He arrived safely at school. His teacher told him not to worry.
Then —
Returning home, he constantly stopped to look for the bear. He never again enjoyed a slow walk from his school.

CONTENT

7 Sentence Power

Whether you are writing stories or nonfiction, you will add interest and clarity if you vary your sentence patterns and types.

Sentence Patterns

The typical sentence begins with the subject. As you examine the following four variations on the same sentence, note how each begins with something other than the subject.

After the thief crept into the room, he stole the television.
Creeping into the room, the thief stole the television.
Into the room the thief crept before he stole the television.
Quietly creeping into the room, the thief stole the television.

Take a closer look at the different patterns in the sentences:

• The first begins with a subordinate clause: "After the thief crept into the room"
• The second begins with a participle, an –ing word: "Creeping"
• The third begins with a phrase: "Into the room"
• The fourth begins with an adverb (often a –ly word): "Quietly"

Sentence Starters

Words that Can Begin Subordinate Clauses	Examples of Participles	Examples of Prepositions	Examples of Adverbs
When	Running	On	Slowly
After	Aiding	In	Quickly
Although	Creeping	After	Sneakily
Before	Descending	Near	Belatedly
Since	Hoping	Into	Swiftly
Unless	Opening	From	Happily
Because	Being	By	Sadly
If	Singing	Across	Drearily
Until	Straying	Below	Reluctantly
While	Assisting	Over	Willingly

Sentence Types

Story writers typically incorporate these different sentence types in their writing to add variety to their writing.

- Most sentences that you write are declarative; that is, they state or declare something. "I'm here today" is a declarative sentence.
- Sentences that pose a question are interrogative: "Will you be here today?"
- Sentences that express emotion are exclamatory: "I am excited to be here today!"
- Sentences that give an order or command are imperative: "Be here today."

Notice the punctuation that ends each of the sentence types: a period for declarative and imperative sentences, an exclamation point for exclamatory sentences, and a question mark for interrogative sentences.

For other strategies related to Sentence Structure, see Revision that Works on page 24 and Sharing Your Story on page 25.

Short Sentence Power

When writers wish to suggest quick action in a descriptive part of their story, they use a series of short sentences. This example captures the action of a popular sport.

> Wood cracks on leather. Cleats dig in. The batter lunges. The shortstop spins. He bobs for the ball. He hurls it to first. The batter's shoe touches. The ball snaps in the glove. Safe!

Action Plan

1. Reread a published story to locate a passage that features varied sentence types and/or sentence patterns. Locate a passage that suggests quick action through a series of short sentences.
2. Use the chart of Sentence Starters to compose
   - three sentences beginning with a subordinate clause
   - three sentences beginning with a participle, or –ing word
   - three sentences beginning with a preposition
   - three sentences beginning with an adverb, often a –ly word
3. Revise a story of your own to include different sentence types and patterns. Use a sticky note or highlighter to mark one or two non-declarative sentences, and one or two sentences that begin with something other than the subject.
4. Revise a story of your own that describes quick action. Use a series of short sentences to suggest the movement.

SENTENCE STRUCTURE

8   Words As Illustrations

Readers of stories visualize the story as they read. They run the movie in their minds by imagining the characters and the events. Words are the illustrations that help readers imagine the story. What do you see in your mind as you read the following sentences?

> The sailor went into the restaurant.
> The weary sailor went into the restaurant.
> The weary sailor staggered into the restaurant.
> The weary sailor staggered into the crowded restaurant.

The adjective "weary" helps you picture the sailor's appearance. The word "staggered" helps you visualize his movement. Another adjective, "crowded" helps you imagine the restaurant precisely. Without the adjective, you might picture an empty restaurant. If you wanted to paint a more complete picture of the sailor's staggering, you would use an adverb:

> The weary sailor clumsily staggered into the crowded restaurant.

Take a look at this story titled "Creak–Bang–Thud." At the numbered places, the student writer decided to brighten two words and add two words.

Creak–Bang–Thud

I could hear owls ① <u>calling</u> me to enter the old house. After a minute of reflection, I decided to go in.

As I opened the door, a wave of ② _____ odors reached my nose. From my pocket I produced a nose clip which I quickly put on. ③ _____ I stood still because a huge crack was coming toward me. When it reached me, the ground beneath me shattered with a bang.

As I fell aimlessly, I could feel the walls closing in on me. Before I knew it, I landed on the amazingly soft floor with a thud. I ④ <u>felt around</u> for my knapsack. Fear spread through my body when I realized it wasn't there. Fear changed to reality when my knapsack landed on my head. I picked it up, reached in and took out a flashlight. As I turned it on, I realized why the floor was so soft. It was pure gold dust. When I looked around I saw a treasure chest. Then I realized I had no way out, until I saw the trap door. I stuffed my pockets with gold and silver, opened the trap door and ran like crazy until I arrived home. I will never have to ask for an allowance again.

Vocabulary Choices

Read the story to consider changes and additions you would make.

① "calling" could be changed to _____

② _____ could be added

③ _____ could be added

④ "felt around" could be changed to_____

In the story "Creak–Bang–Thud":

The student writer changed

① "calling to "taunting"
④ "felt around" to "groped"

The student added

② "foul-smelling"
③ "Horrified"

The changes and additions have added color to the story for the reader to picture the scene more effectively. You probably suggested other possibilities, and so the scene your reader pictures will be slightly different from the one in the mind of the reader of the original writer's story. Your word choices also contribute to your voice as a writer. You separate yourself from other writers by using words that add color as only you can (see Voice on page 20).

A few well-considered changes and additions can definitely add value to your writing. But long lists of adjectives or adverbs, such as "the joyful, chatty, naughty, unfocused child," make for overdone descriptions. Your rule should be to add colorful words only if they help the reader picture the text more clearly. If the words do not add important detail, delete them. Note the helpful revision in this excerpt from a student's story.

Long ago there lived a dragon — a very mean, diabolical, evil, selfish, greedy and gluttonous dragon.
Became
Long ago there lived a dragon — a very selfish and gluttonous dragon.

Action Plan

1. Reread a published story. Note three examples of colorful word choices that improve the reader's ability to visualize the story.
2. Revise one of your own stories:
   • Brighten at least two words
   • Add one or two effective adjectives or adverbs
3. If your story already features colorful vocabulary, note your effective word choices.

9 Writing With a Distinctive Voice

You may have heard that voice is a desirable characteristic in your story writing. How do you add voice to your writing? When you include relevant details that other writers miss, and when your word choices and comparisons are original, your writing has a voice that's all your own — a personal touch that distinguishes you from other writers.

Originality is not the only feature that lends voice to writing. Honesty is important. So is your effort to capture oral language as it is actually spoken by people. Still, focusing on originality is one practical and effective method to strengthen the voice in your writing.

While you may not consider yourself to be particularly imaginative, you can intensify voice in your writing through two specific strategies:

- Add at least one original comparison.
- Add details based on first-hand observation.

Original Comparisons

Clichés — overused expressions and comparisons — are the greatest enemy of voice in writing. Expressions like "dark as night," "like a bump on a log," or "ugly as sin" are examples of clichés: they have lost their power through overuse.

Showing, Not Telling on page 13 suggests that, instead of mentioning an emotion such as joy or fear, you will add value to your story by including details that show the emotion. You will add even more to that richness by taking at least one of your details to create an original comparison.

Remember that original comparisons can be effective even when they are not tied to emotion. For instance, you could add original comparisons for descriptions of setting and character. Still, if you are striving to add voice to your writing, showing rather than telling emotion and working to create an original comparison are practical and manageable strategies, especially if you feel that your writing tends to be wooden.

Notice how these comparisons from student work convey an emotion in an imaginative way. What emotion is being shown?

I smiled a half-moon smile. _____

My eyes opened as wide as avocado pits. _____

The player's movement to the left and the right was quick and swift like random lightning bolts. _____

He was as hungry as a bear who had just awakened from hibernation. _____

Extending a Comparison

Consider other extensions to the "hungry as …." comparison.
- hungry as a lion that _____
- hungry as someone who _____
- hungry as _____

Use the Comparison Frame to help you extend familiar comparisons, and add voice to your writing.

John was as frustrated as the star hockey forward who has not scored in ten games.

Their conversation boomed like the noise in the school hallway that clearly signals the start of summer break.

Comparison Frame

_____ as/like _____

who/that_____

For other strategies related to Vocabulary, see Revision that Works on page 24 and Publishing Your Story on page 25. For other strategies related to Voice, see Journal Writing Focused on Conflict on page 12; Words As Illustrations on page 18; Revision that Works on page 24; and Sharing Your Story on page 25.

Descriptive Details

Another way to add voice is to include descriptive details that others might overlook. The best way to do this is through first-hand observations.

For example, if your character is lost in a crowded mall, don't just imagine the crowded mall to write about it. Visit a crowded mall with notepad in hand. What details will help your reader see and feel what the character feels? Write down those details. Watch carefully to note details that others might overlook. By including relevant, original details, you add voice and value to your story.

Action Plan

1. In a favorite published story, identify a passage where the author's voice comes through strongly. What features add voice to the passage?
2. Locate a place in one of your stories where you could add one original comparison. Add the comparison and read the passage again, noting how it affects the voice of the passage.
3. Locate a place in your story that would benefit from the addition of descriptive detail. Use first-hand observation to note and add details that others might miss.

VOCABULARY AND VOICE

10 Usage and Spelling

Have you ever had something funny, strange, or deeply emotional happen to you, and then messed it up completely when you try to tell it as a story to someone else? In story writing, your story will be successful only if the reader can understand what you're trying to say. You have learned rules for spelling, grammar, punctuation, and word use, but always remember that the rules are there so that what you have written makes sense to the reader.

For example, how does the following sentence confuse the reader?

Mary told Irene that she did well in the mathematics test.

We're not sure whether the "she" refers to Mary or Irene. Reference books on writing would label the problem as "unclear pronoun reference." A writer should rewrite such a sentence so that the reader is not distracted or confused.

Usage

The word "usage" means the standard way that a group of people use language. When we employ the standard system for punctuation, capitalization, spelling, and sentence construction, we communicate more clearly and efficiently. Many people use the word "grammar" to mean usage, but you don't have to worry too much about this distinction. The important point is that you respect standard usage in your writing.

This chart illustrates a few of the most common matters of standard usage.

Some Commonly Misused Words	Some Capitalization and Punctuation Problems
• affect/effect • accept/except • can/may • bad/badly • principle/principal • could of (should be *could have*) • lie/lay • irregardless (should be *regardless* or *irrespective*) • there/their/they're	• lack of capital letters for proper nouns • lack of a capital letter to begin a sentence • lack of capital letters for important words in titles • improper punctuation to end sentences (period/question mark/exclamation point) • improper use of colons and semicolons • incorrect placement of commas

Some Sentence Structure Problems	Some Commonly Misspelled Words
• lack of subject–verb agreement • sentence fragments • run-on sentences • wordy sentences • unclear pronoun reference • misplaced modifiers • lack of parallel structure	• dinning (should be *dining*) • wierd (should be *weird*) • recieve (should be *receive*) • preformance (should be *performance*) • cafateria (should be *cafeteria*) • ocassion (should be *occasion*) • hieght (should be *height*)

For other strategies related to Conventions, see Revision that Works on page 24 and Sharing Your Story on page 25.

Using Reference Books

Your teacher will recommend reference books that will answer your questions about standard English usage. Check these books when you are unsure.

When drafting a story, many writers write the letter *U* above a section of their writing when they are unsure about usage, and an *S* above a word when they are unsure of spelling. They can go back to check on the items later.

Remember that spell-checkers and grammar-checkers in word-processing programs have their limitations. Spell-checkers will not catch commonly confused words, such as "affect" and "effect." And they won't catch many typographical errors, such as "won" for "own." Some grammar-checkers signal a problem in usage when there is none. You still need to proofread.

Employ the following strategies to improve your standard English usage:

- Check a reference book or a dictionary when you are unsure.
- Complete practice exercises recommended by your teacher to improve your understanding of standard usage
- Complete a goals chart (see page 28) especially for usage goals.
- Keep a personal Spelling Demons list for words you frequently misspell.
- Include a check for your usage and spelling problems in the revision stage of your writing. (See Revision on page 24.)

Spelling Demons

Your Spelling Demons list should be the first page of the Spelling section of your writing folder or binder. Take responsibility for improvement of your spelling by thinking about strategies that will help you learn correct spelling. Many students report success with a three-step strategy.

Three-Step Spelling Strategy

1. Copy out the misspelled word with the misspelled part circled.
2. Close your eyes and imagine the word correctly spelled. Write out the correctly spelled word five times.
3. Rewrite the sentence in which the misspelled word occurred. This time, spell the word correctly.

Action Plan

1. Keep a Personal Writing Goals (see page 28) record in your writing folder or binder.
2. Keep a Spelling Demons list in your writing folder or binder.
3. Use the Three-Step Spelling Strategy for each of your spelling demons.
4. **Test Strategy**: Ensure that you plan for usage and spelling checks when you write a story under test conditions. Sometimes testing procedures allow you to use dictionaries and reference books as well as spell- and grammar-checkers on word-processing programs. Remember to write on every second line; that way you can complete your corrections and improvements efficiently when you do not have time to rewrite your story.

CONVENTIONS

11 Revision that Works

Researchers into student writing have established the power of revising writing with specific criteria, like the ones suggested in this book.

- My story presents essential narrative detail for the reader — a main character, a setting, a conflict, a resolution, an ending. (See page 14.)
- All details, including dialogue, directly develop the story's central conflict. (See pages 12, 14.)
- My story's point of view works effectively. (See page 7.)
- The beginning of my story commands attention. (See page 9.)
- The ending of my story points to a theme. (See page 10.)
- I show emotion rather than tell about it. (See page 13.)
- My story includes details based on first-hand observation.
- My story contains at least one original comparison. (See page 21.)
- My story contains several precise and colorful words to help my reader visualize details. (See page 18.)
- My story contains varied sentences types and patterns. (See page 16.)
- I employ a series of short sentences to suggest quick action when it is needed. (See page 17.)
- I have edited my story for specific points of usage such as standard capitalization, standard punctuation, and clear pronoun reference. (See page 22.)
- I have edited my story for correct spelling. (See page 23.)

You should not try to improve all of these features at one time; be focused in your revisions. Choose a few criteria related to your current story writing goals.

An acronym can make it easier to recall revision criteria. Students familiar with the strategies in this book created the BOSS-DEW checklist shown here.

BOSS-DEW

B = Beginning	Does it capture attention?	☐
O = Original comparisons	Does the story have at least one?	☐
S = Showing not telling	Does the story show rather than tell emotion?	☐
S = Sentence structure	Does the story have varied sentences?	☐
D = Demons	Have I checked for personal spelling/usage demons?	☐
E = Ending	Have I checked that it points to a theme?	☐
W = Words	Have I added color to at least three words?	☐

Action Plan

1. Use a highlighter or sticky note to mark a part of your story where you have succeeded in meeting a specific criterion. Use different colors for different criteria to help you see where you need to add, delete, or change something.

2. **Test Strategy:**
   - Draft your story on every second line — revisions will be easier to make, and the result will be easier to read.
   - Check if you are allowed to use word-processing to make revisions.

12 Sharing Your Story

Share your stories with classmates, friends, and family. Not only will their responses help you improve your story writing, but they will affirm and encourage you as a writer.

Sharing Aloud

When you have the opportunity to read your story to others, be sure to read it well. Keep the following tips in mind:

- Respect punctuation cues. Pause for commas. Stop for periods. Show emotion at exclamation points; use an inquisitive tone of voice for question marks.
- Decide about timing and pacing.
- Think about your volume.
- Decide about emphasis. A slight pause before you read an important point and a slight increase in volume as you read it will signal that listeners should pay particular attention.

Sometimes you will request feedback. Begin by asking your readers or listeners to tell you what they liked about your story. Stories don't work when details are not clear; therefore, ask if anyone has questions. Finally, ask for a *single* suggestion: work on one goal at a time.

Story Sharing

1. What do you like about my story?
2. Do you have a question about my story?
3. Please offer a suggestion to help me improve this story.

Publishing Your Story

Publishing stories is an important form of sharing. Publishing at school takes several forms:

- Reading your story to classmates or other students
- Posting your stories in classrooms and hallways
- Printing stories in school newsletters, yearbooks, and class and school anthologies of writing

The skills that you have developed to improve your story writing are worthy of praise and celebration.

Getting Your Story Published

See page 7 for two publications that include the work of young story writers. Watch for other publications that invite submissions from student writers. Use the sharing that you do in your school to consider whether other audiences in and beyond your community might enjoy reading your story or hearing you read it to them.

Action Plan

1. Use the three-point Story Sharing strategy to present your story to a classmate, friend, or family member.
2. Publish at least one of your stories at school. Consider whether you wish to seek publication beyond your school.

REVISING AND SHARING

Supporting Student Story Writers

12 Sides to Your Story...

- will have optimum benefit for students when teachers emphasize flexible use of the resource, when they set instructional priorities for their students' story writing, when they implement principles of differentiated instruction, and when they emphasize the reading/writing connection.

- may be used by students in two viable ways: to set and achieve goals to improve their story writing; or to follow a story writing process that has worked for other student writers. Student flexibility with the resource intensifies its usefulness. Students requiring advice about the story writing process will typically begin with Writing Variables for Stories (page 6), and move on to Planning Strategies for Story Writing (page 14), Story Beginnings that Command Attention (page 9), and Story Endings that Point to Theme (page 10). They may refer to other sections once they have completed their first draft.

- emphasizes that success in story writing rests on students' understanding of critical story elements: character, conflict, rising action, resolution, ending. As a result, teachers often choose story organization as a priority until students demonstrate control in their story writing. Some students struggle with story structure in their writing. Once they demonstrate control of story structure in their writing, they are ready for a shift of instructional priorities to other matters such as Showing, Not Telling (page 13) and Writing with a Distinctive Voice (page 20).

- can support teachers in employing differentiated instruction to help students learn about critical story elements. Kinesthetic learners benefit from acting out stories with related discussion about story elements. Auditory learners benefit from storytelling in the classroom, also with related discussion about story elements. Visual learners benefit from sketching story plans as they focus on critical story elements.

- stresses the reading/writing connection to help students improve their story writing. Noting how published writers and successful student writers structure stories and employ a range of techniques clearly benefits students in their own story writing.

- has been designed to help students transform ordinary story writing into extraordinary story writing. Flexible use of the resource based on instructional priorities, and on differentiated instruction with an emphasis on the reading/writing connection, will help more students succeed in story writing more often.

Strategy Checklist

- ☐ I use journal writing to consider how people deal with problems or conflicts.

- ☐ Before I plan my story, I consider important writing variables — role, audience, format, topic, and purpose.

- ☐ Before I write, I consider critical story elements like main character, conflict, rising action, climax, ending.

- ☐ My story's beginning creates interest.

- ☐ My story's ending suggests a theme.

- ☐ When I write about emotion or build suspense, I "show rather than tell."

- ☐ My story contains unique details and original comparisons: original metaphors, similes, and other word-pictures.

- ☐ I include specific, colorful words that help readers visualize my story.

- ☐ I vary sentence types and patterns, and use short sentences to suggest quick action.

- ☐ I check reference books to correct mistakes I frequently make in spelling, punctuation, capitalization, and grammar/usage.

- ☐ I revise my writing to check for features such as word choice, varied sentence patterns, or a beginning that creates interest.

- ☐ I regularly share my stories with audiences other than my teacher.

My Personal Writing Goals

Goals Identified	Goals Achieved

Story Frame

Somebody —

Somewhere —

Wanted —

But —

Showing the problem —

So —

Then —